++ Si
Simon
Cats

D1254976

OCT. 1 4 2002   AP 27 '11
APR
MR 09
MR 14 '88   MY 20 '9   AP 1 '95   NO 27 '96
AP 11 '8   JA 25 '97
      SE 30 '9   JE 19 '95   MAR. 0 4 1997
AP 13 '88   NO 04 '9   SE 12 '95   JE 24 '97
MY 04 '88
          OC 12 '92   SE 29 '95   AG 05 '97
JY 01 '88   NO 20 '95   FE 16 '98
AG 16 '88   FE 01 '93   DE 04 '95   JE 02 '98
         AG 05 '98   FE 08 '99
MR 23 '89   SE 22 '93   JA 30 '98   MAR. 2 5 2000
AP 20 '89   DE 28 '93
MY 25 89   SE 26 '94   MR 14 '96   JAN. 2 6 2002
FE 1 '90   MY 28 '96   FEB. 2 0 2002
AG 07 '90   OC 11 '94   JE 07 '96   MAR. 2 0 2002

                                  SEP. 4   2002

DEMCO

Cats Do, Dogs Don't

Norma Simon
pictures by Dora Leder

ALBERT WHITMAN & COMPANY, NILES, ILLINOIS

Also by Norma Simon, illustrated by Dora Leder
I Know What I Like
I'm Busy, Too
I Was So Mad
Nobody's Perfect, Not Even My Mother
Oh, That Cat!
Where Does My Cat Sleep?
Why Am I Different?

Library of Congress Cataloging-in-Publication Data

Simon, Norma.
   Cats do, dogs don't.
   Summary: Contrasts, using simple examples, the many
differences between dogs and cats.
   1. Dogs—Juvenile literature. 2. Cats—Juvenile
literature. 3. Dogs—Behavior—Juvenile literature.
4. Cats—Behavior—Juvenile literature. 1. [Cats.
2. Dogs.] I. Leder, Dora, ill. II. Title.
SF426.5S545 1986   646.7'0887   86-5618
ISBN 0-8075-1102-1

Text © 1986 by Norma Simon
Illustrations © 1986 by Dora Leder
Published in 1986 by Albert Whitman & Company,
Niles, Illinois
Published simultaneously in Canada by General
Publishing, Limited, Toronto
Printed in U.S.A. All rights reserved.
10   9   8   7   6   5   4   3   2   1

*To Ed, with love, for inspiration
and generous contribution to our book*
N.S.

For Ed and Kearse
D.L.

Dogs can jump up
and catch a Frisbee.
Did you ever see a cat do that?

Cats can jump up on fences
and walk along the tops.
Dogs can't do that.

Cats lick themselves to keep clean.

Not dogs! You have to give them shampoos.

Dogs will bring you your slippers.

Cats won't bring you anything (but things they've caught).

Dogs dig holes to bury their bones.
They dig them up later to gnaw on
and carry around in their mouths.
Cats never bury bones.

Cats act silly when they sniff catnip.
Dogs don't care what it smells like.

Cats climb high on rooftops
and up into the trees.
They cry, "MEEEE-OWWWW!"
when they can't get down.
Dogs can't climb even if they try.

Dogs bark when people come to your house,
but I never saw a "Watch Cat." Did you?

Cats eat only what they need.
Then they stop.

If you give dogs too much food,
they'll eat it all up.
(Then, sometimes, they'll get sick.)

Cats can stay alone in the house
when you visit your aunt overnight.
They use a litter box as their toilet.

Dogs can't stay alone.
You have to walk them every day and every night.

Some dogs love to swim in a lake.
They jump and splash all over you.

Most cats hate water.
My cat won't even walk on the beach!

Cats sharpen their claws on trees
and, sometimes, on Mom's sofa.
I'm glad dogs don't do that.

Dogs know when they've done something bad.
They look ashamed.
Cats never look ashamed about what they do.

Cats never chase cars or bicycles,
but lots of dogs do.

Cats chase toy mice
and pounce on pieces of string
when you wiggle them back and forth.
Wind-up toys and jiggly strings
don't excite dogs.

Dogs race you to the school bus stop
and wait for you to come home.

Some cats pretend they don't care when you come home.
They don't run over to say, "Hi!"

Cats flick their tails
when they're angry or scared.
They hiss and spit
and hunch their backs.

Dogs growl and bare their teeth
to show they're mad.

Cats purr-r-r- when they're happy.

Dogs wag their tails.

They're both happy when they're with you.
For though cats and dogs are different,
both love you,
and need you,
and want you to love them back.